ABANDONED MONTANA

FROM BOOM TO BUST

BASTIEN GRANDY

America Through Time is an imprint of Fonthill Media LLC
www.through-time.com
office@through-time.com

Published by Arcadia Publishing by arrangement with Fonthill Media LLC
For all general information, please contact Arcadia Publishing:
Telephone: 843-853-2070
Fax: 843-853-0044
E-mail: sales@arcadiapublishing.com
For customer service and orders:
Toll-Free 1-888-313-2665

www.arcadiapublishing.com

First published 2022

Copyright © Bastien Grandy 2022

ISBN 978-1-63499-411-8

Typeset in Trade Gothic 10pt on 15pt
Printed and bound in England

CONTENTS

ABOUT THE AUTHOR

BASTIEN GRANDY is an adventurer and photographer. He has spent most of his time traveling the state of Montana looking for eerie and historical places to photograph. He enjoys the worn character in things that came before him. In his downtime, he continues his joy of history and fixes up classic cars, antique guitars, and vintage cameras. He is planning to attend Montana State University in the fall of 2022.

[*Photo by Colten Grandy*]

PREFACE

Buried deep in the undergrowth, about half a mile into the trees behind the home of Remi Mouledous (my cousin of sorts), sits a very dilapidated old cabin. It has no roof, no doors, and no windows, but to a bunch of young adventurous kids, it was just waiting to be explored. Remi and I, along with a myriad of our friends, made a slew of forts out of the cabin or excavated around it with broken shovels in hopes of finding historical artifacts—which turned out to be, more often than not, rusty nails. As we outgrew our lopsided hut, we began exploring the nearby area. We crawled through barbed wire fences and blissfully ignored "no trespassing" signs. Between the properties of our families and friends, we had so much to explore. We ventured into small, deserted cabins or walked a couple of paces into the mouth of a collapsed mine. For me, it was all for the allure of adventure, an adventure that had been instilled in me by the excellent stories of my relatives. Whether it was a great feat or simply a common occurrence, every story was fantastical to me. I found childish delight in family visits to local ghost towns or my frequent hikes to an abandoned homestead near my grandparents' cabin.

I'm certainly not the only one, though. Exploring decrepit shanties while deep in the woods on a hiking expedition is a uniquely Montanan experience. Childhood stories of playing in derelict old cars or climbing onto rusty farm equipment are simply common tales from the residents of the Big Sky State.

Maybe that is the beauty of Montana, the cycle of stories, inspirations, and adventures. Whether it's a grandfather that tells of rodeo tales, ultimately inspiring one of his kin to take up a similar sport; or a family friend that speaks of wild shenanigans in a band, causing a kid to pick up the guitar; everyone has their stories, inspirations, and adventures. I was inspired by the stories of those who came before me. My adventure, as I see it, is exploring the places of my ancestors.

Remi and I share this adventure. As we grew older, these locations would become frequent destinations for our weekend adventures. We ventured far outside of our family backyards to see what was left by those who came before us. We began to appreciate the creaky floorboards, the little bits of moss that poked between the bricks, every bit of character and charm. A building, in and of itself, is a man-made thing, but these buildings existed in a delicate alliance between nature and mankind. Every photo matters, and every detail is important. Our duty to these structures is to photograph their subtle stories before the buildings return to the soil from whence they came.

INTRODUCTION

In Montana, the only thing that is richer than its mountains are the stories it holds. Stories passed down around blazing campfires outside of family cabins. Stories of land so plentiful in gold that one could shake sagebrush and come home with a week's wages. Stories of fantastic gun-slinging outlaws meeting an untimely fate at the end of a vigilante's noose. Fantastic tales drive each and every Montanan. They drove people to come to the Treasure State and kept them interested generation after generation.

To be a third or fourth generation Montanan is an honor. To know that one's grandparents crossed the United States on homesteading wagon trains or came from foreign lands seeking their fortune in the mines gives a small sense of pride. The history under the Big Sky is vast, and the knowledge that one's ancestors contributed to it, however small of a contribution, ties every Montanan together. Montana, at its core, is a state of trailblazers. The prospectors that once panned its rivers and cut through its mountains or the homesteaders that tilled its land and sowed its fields have both made a lasting and important impact on Montana. While their additions to Montana's past may sit rotting in fields or rusting away amongst sprouting weeds, they appeal to the curiosity of many Montanans. Off-kilter wooden headframes surrounded by a myriad of shacks and shanties sit just out of reach behind rotting fence posts and a no-trespassing sign. Odd grain silos and barns litter the hillsides beside bustling highways. The occasional historical info sign will grace the oppressive chain-link fences surrounding an old substation or a crumbling general store, briefly echoing a cautionary tale if one were to succumb to their curiosity and cross their imposing iron barrier. To most, the museum visit is enough to ward off these thoughts. Browsing historical artifacts and reading plaques certainly satisfies the desire for knowledge, but for a person who wishes to truly experience history, one must venture over their barriers to where the history itself occurred. No prospectors roamed the exhibits of the museum and no outlaws robbed from the wagons in its halls. Rather, one must go where time has stood still and where Mother Nature is the only visitor.

In most cases, they have not changed since they were abandoned so many decades ago. Their halls sit forsaken and their rooms vacant. For me, I still feel a certain sense of connection with the building's previous inhabitants. A memo on a paper scrap or a plate of rancid decade-old food paints a humble picture of those who once lived within the now tarnished walls. The boogeyman that might have once haunted the children whose desks sit deserted tends to appear again in shadows as I creep through forlorn halls. I do not walk fearlessly, however, and I must caution other explorers to the many problems. The unknown darkness or the possibility of being discovered by an irate proprietor are both tremendous worries. On top of that, the danger of possibly plummeting down a mineshaft or falling through a collapsed floor are all formidable fears. If I keep these in mind and watch my step, I am always rewarded with a little tidbit buried in rubble. Each artifact or discovery paints the picture of a story that slowly unfolds in front of me. *Abandoned Montana: From Boom to Bust* aims to display these forgotten stories and extend the sense of awe I felt as a beholder of such bleak elegance. I can wonder what is behind a door, or underneath a rusty hatch, but there is one thing that I know for certain: I am one of those peculiar souls that wish to experience history through the forlorn and forgotten.

1

COMET

Approximately six miles northwest of Boulder, MT, Comet, named after the Comet Mine, was founded in 1883. In 1874, John W. Russell filed for a patent on the Comet Lode, not long before being bought by the Alta-Montana Company. The town flourished under the prosperity of the Comet Mine. The greater Comet area grew rapidly, with its population ballooning to 300 people. It boasted more than twenty saloons and approximately ninety buildings overall. For the booming mine, a new aerial tramway, hoists, and water pumps were added following investment from the Helena Mining and Reduction Company.

Regrettably, Comet's good fortune couldn't last forever. By 1887, the mine was shuttered, as the vast majority of precious metals had already been extracted. For a lengthy period, Comet was a ghost town. Tides turned in 1926 when the Basin Montana Tunnel Company acquired the mine and turned the focus towards base metals, like zinc, copper, and lead, of which the mine still had a wealth of. By the 1930s, Comet had been called "the largest mining venture in Montana outside of Butte".[1] At this time, the mine employed fifty men, each making an average of five dollars a day. Despite the prosperity, Comet's ghost town status descended upon it once again, permanently this time, when the majority of the townsfolk left for WWII. Ultimately, the Comet Mine produced twenty million dollars in gold, silver, lead, zinc, and copper. Today, of the previous 300 residents, three remain. The buildings sit in various degrees of disarray, most missing any semblance of a roof or walls. In comparison, the mine and bunkhouse buildings sit relatively unphased due to the metal construction. Shacks litter the countryside, yet fewer and fewer remain every couple of years. It is only a matter of time before they are reduced to rubble through the passing of time.

Left: An abandoned wooden headframe overlooks a series of hills. Only parts of the original minecart track are left. The lopsided structure is missing much of its necessary lumber.

Below: This old barn sits directly in front of the main road going through Comet. A dilapidated couch is the only thing inside.

Above left: There is a road that splits off the main road leading to this small house. Pictured is the view towards the back door.

Above right: One of the most iconic buildings in Comet is this hotel. Most of the floors and roof have caved in, leaving just a shell.

Left: A chair sits alone in an otherwise empty room. This picture was taken during a visit to Comet during the wintertime.

Below: A beautiful house with green painted walls is just up a hill from the main road. The house's walls are ready to collapse.

Just in front of the aforementioned house, there are remnants of an old truck. The Comet mill is visible in the distance.

Here is a view of the Comet Mine's mill during the summertime. There is a very calm stream that runs in front of the mine and through the valley.

Left: A small mountain road leads up to the mill. The road itself is obscured by trees.

Below: The mountain road leads under an outcropping in the topmost part of the mill. On the concrete foundation are graffiti tags and artwork.

Right: An old engine sits in the opening of a large garage of sorts, although it may have served a different purpose during the mine's operation.

Below: The mill stairsteps down the hill. In one of these levels lies an old locker for miners and graffiti artwork. This particular section is the only one with stairs that have not been removed.

The mill has seen better days. The rubble of what was once a roof and walls now lies on the floor.

2

ELKHORN

A wealth of silver deposits were discovered eight miles northeast of Boulder, early in 1870. Their discoverer, Peter Wyes, faced an early and mysterious death. Not a year later, a wealthy Virginia City magnate, Anton M. Holter, swooped in and purchased Wyes' claim. By 1875, Holter had opened what would become the district's largest mine, Elkhorn, and soon a town would form bearing the mine's name.

Eventually, the magnitude of ore would outweigh the processing capabilities of Elkhorn's ore mill and the mine was shuttered in 1881. The next year, operations would be resumed under the direction of the Elkhorn Mining Company, which was quick to improve the insufficient mill. In 1890, the Sherman Silver Purchase Act ushered Elkhorn into a golden age. The population skyrocketed to 2,500 people, largely due to the vast number of immigrant families that settled in the area.

Elkhorn was vast. An array of homes dotted the hillsides and valleys. The town boasted a bowling alley, multiple hotels, saloons, and much more. The will of the town was weathered, however, as a result of a harsh diphtheria epidemic that claimed dozens of children's lives throughout 1888 and 1889. Luck would further desert the town as Elkhorn's silver veins became exhausted. As a result, the mine went through a series of brief ownerships over the next couple of decades. In 1931, the discontinuation of the railroad service was the final nail in the coffin and eventually led to the closing of the mine in 1937. Over the lifetime of the Elkhorn Mine, it produced fourteen million dollars in silver.

Elkhorn as a town still lives on, with many of the original families still residing there today. Many shacks and rubble from what used to be houses stand in between fully functioning households. The skeleton of the old Elkhorn mine is visible to the town's inhabitants as a reminder of hope and hardship.

Above: The interior of the Fraternity Hall in Elkhorn, one of few remaining original buildings, has only a couch and a couple of chairs on the first floor.

Left: A building of an unknown purpose has caved in to the Elkhorn mine. Many other wooden buildings nearby have succumbed to a similar fate.

Above: Some maintenance buildings sit at the top of a hill. The headframe, which is out of frame, is nearby. Each building has boxes of replacement parts inside.

Right: The red brick building has piles of old cans and a tire, in addition to the boxes.

The Elkhorn Mine's headframe is relatively small and made of wood. Most of the front of the headframe has collapsed into the shaft.

This is the view from the top of the hill, right in front of the headframe. To the right, there are the remnants of the platform that led to the mill.

The headframe sits just a bit away from its control building. The surrounding support structures, powerlines, and tracks are surprisingly intact.

Left: A brick structure sits on a steep hill. It was likely a chimney or stack of some sort.

Below: The Elkhorn mill is in ruin. The stone foundations are intact and can still be seen, but the walls and roofs have fallen apart.

This building has caved in upon itself, allowing one to see a lone pine.

This is one of many foundations in the area. In this foundation lies scrap and stove parts.

3

CASTLE TOWN

In 1882, Hanson Barnes discovered rich deposits of silver and lead just thirteen miles southeast of White Sulphur Springs. Almost overnight, more than 1,000 claims had been filed and multiple mines erected. What would become the largest mine in the district, the Cumberland was erected in 1884 by Lafe Hensley. Months later, the town of Castle was born. Its population quickly grew to 2,000 and many new buildings were constructed. However small Castle seemed, it still had as many as seven brothels and fourteen saloons. It didn't just attract rowdy bachelors, though. The famous gun-slinging frontierswoman Calamity Jane had briefly attempted to establish a restaurant there, but it was not meant to be.

As the town grew larger, one crippling shortcoming became glaringly apparent: the price of moving anything to and from town was extraordinarily expensive, due to the lack of a railroad. Castle had made do in previous years, but the necessary volume of coke, the fuel used for Castle's smelters, had grown greatly during the silver boom, causing great strain on profitability. In 1892, a railroad investor by the name of Richard Austin Harlow moved to lay track towards Castle through the Big Belt Mountains. By 1897, a track had been laid, but it was four years too late. The silver panic of 1893 caused an extreme devaluation of silver, and the ore that mine owners had been hoarding in anticipation of the railroad was now nearly worthless. Most silver mines closed for good, with lead mines meeting a similar fate months later due to dropping lead prices. By the 1930s, the last of the town's stubborn inhabitants had deserted their homes. Today, the buildings are, for the most part, rubble and foundations. Any structures that still stand remain as grey skeletons of saloons, hotels, and homes, wind whistling dryly through open slats.

Above: Two small cabins sit just up the hill from the main road leading to Castle Town. Both seem to have been used as a shelter for grazing cattle.

Right: A rear view of the distant cabin in the last picture. This cabin seems to have had an expansion at one point that has since collapsed.

A small shed or barn is just in front of a cabin.

The sun sits directly above what is left of Castle Town. Four buildings are visible in this shot. Not a single building has doors or glass, and only a couple have complete walls.

Above left: Another cabin can be seen from the top floor of the frontmost cabin in the previous picture. The floor leading to this window is littered with holes.

Above right: This is the view from a window on the opposite side of the same cabin. Many similar cabins dot the area.

A lot of names are carved in the plaster of the buildings. At a glance, names went as far back as 1959.

Left: Most of the plaster has since weathered away in the buildings. Sometimes, not even wooden slats are left on the walls.

Below: An overhang is on the verge of collapse. A small house is connected to this structure

Above: Here is another view of the far cabins that were previously seen through a window.

Right: The interior of one of the cabins is full of light. The floorboards are full of cracks and holes.

The covered porch is barely covered now and sits completely off-kilter. The cabin itself has only one section of roof remaining.

A couple of rectangular stone foundations can be seen from a passing road. They are all in a line. Possibly, they were a part of a mill at one point.

4

MILWAUKEE RAILROAD PACIFIC EXTENSION

The greater the production of Montana's industries, the greater the need for the railroad. By the 1890s, the Chicago, Milwaukee, and St. Paul railroad, also known as the Milwaukee Road, had to remain competitive with other lines and decided to survey an extension to the Pacific. In 1905, the 2,300 miles of track were approved by the board for sixty million dollars. The Pacific Extension was completed in 1909, making it one of two other transcontinental railroads to pass through Montana. Due to the difficulty of operating steam locomotives in certain sections of the Milwaukee, large parts of the Pacific Extension had to be electrified. The 440-mile section between Harlowton, Montana, and Avery, Idaho, known as the Rocky Mountain Division, was converted in 1916. The 216-mile section between Othello, Washington, and Tacoma, Washington, known as the Coast Division, was converted in 1919. In the United States, the Rocky Mountain Division was the longest electrified line of its time. Electrification required power substations spaced thirty-seven miles apart on the line. The Rocky Mountain Division had fourteen substations in all, and the Coastal Division had thirteen. The Loweth and Ravenna stations, substation numbers two and nine respectively, are the two specific Rocky Mountain Division substations detailed in this book. The Pacific Extension was an engineering marvel, but between the cost of the extension itself and electrification, the Milwaukee Road's debt had grown to 490 million dollars. It would face a series of bankruptcies over the next couple of decades, first in 1928 and again in 1935. After finally breaking through economic turmoil in 1945, the Milwaukee enjoyed a period of prosperity, new luxurious types of locomotives, and expansions of their line. In the 1970s, however, a series of poor decisions, particularly the decision to de-electrify the entirety of the extension and transition to diesel, just as the oil crisis struck the United States, led to the Pacific Extension's demise. After the Milwaukee Road filed for bankruptcy in 1977, the company decided to abandon its western lines. In 1980, the Pacific Extension closed for good. Little is left of the original line. Some substations still are visible on hillsides, but many have been demolished. The line itself is nothing but dirt mounds and rusting railroad signals. The only passengers the Pacific Extension carries are the hikers and explorers that venture on railroad hiking trails and through decaying train tunnels.

Above: When passing through Loweth, between Harlowton and Townsend, one can see substation two off the side of the road.

Right: Here is a closer look at the substation. It is not a small building. The set of double doors is at least ten feet tall.

Above left: The building is full of light. It has a multitude of tall small-paned windows that encompass the entire building. There are also a lot of concrete foundations where machinery once was.

Above right: This doorway leads to a concrete path that goes towards supporting buildings. Most of these buildings are only foundations now, and the corresponding door for the doorway is nowhere to be seen.

This house is the only remaining structure, aside from the substation. The house is in sorry shape, nonetheless.

In the main area of the substation, there is one wall covered in graffiti. There is little to no graffiti anywhere else in this building.

This wood outcropping on the side of the building has seen better days. It has some sort of ladder strapped to the wall.

Usually, these windows are below the water. All the water is frozen at this time of year, leaving the rust on these windows out in the open air.

Above: This train car is in a field across from the substation. Little is left of this poor dilapidated car.

Right: When driving towards Harlowton, many rail signals can be seen off the highway.

This is the view from the top of substation nine, the Ravenna substation. Teenagers of nearby Missoula have constructed a ramp ladder amalgamation to replace the removed rungs of the maintenance ladder, allowing access to the roof.

This is a not-so-abandoned train car in Harlowton, the beginning point for electrification of the Pacific Extension. There used to be a rail spur in Harlowton that led to the next mentioned location.

5

MONTANA FLOUR MILLS CO. FLOUR MILL

Visible just off the highway through Harlowtown, the Montana Flour Mills Co. flour mill stands as a symbol of times past. In 1909, H. B. Eggers, the president of a North Dakotan mill company, awarded a contract of $15,000 to a local Harlowton firm for the construction of the mill. Initially, the mill was expected to employ approximately twenty-five men. Not long after its completion in late 1909, a 1912 addition added a large stone grain elevator to the north side of the mill, along with additional concrete silos, expanding the mill's capabilities and labor needs. These additions certainly did not go to waste, as according to a 1912 Harlowton newspaper, "The Montana Flour Mills Company succeeded in taking first prize at the Montana State Fair for the best flour manufactured in the state."[1]

The Montana Flour Mills Co. flour mill closed after approximately a century in the 2010s. It is now known as the Lode Elevator Co., after a recent change of hands of the grain silo. The current owners have made great strides at getting the site functioning again after a decade of negligence. The building itself has some damage, but it has good bones. The machines that move grain throughout the building are functional and power has been restored, but the machinery used in the actual milling of grain had been stripped out of the building at some point. Maybe one day, the grain silo will operate at full capacity as it did so many decades ago and remind those who live nearby of Harlowton's roots.

Here is the view of the Lode Elevator Company from the nearby road. The current owner has managed to get the power working.

One of the original generators remains in the building.

Above left: This is one of the operation valve wheels underneath the grain silos. Lights are a relief when the previous trip was pitch black.

Above right: An elevator of sorts has platforms as well as places to hold on attached neatly to one revolving belt.

Above left: These two sets of buttons probably controlled nearby machinery.

Above right: Here is one of the many fire doors in the main tower of the building. With the pulley system, the door was surprisingly easy to open and close.

Above left: The interior of the grain silo building is in great shape. This is the third story.

Above right: At the top of the grain silos is an operations building. At the end of this building lies a machine to move the grain.

Above left: Attached to the roof of the operations building is an old industrial hook that can lift 2 tons.

Above right: This is the view from the tower towards the end of the operations building. Machinery goes the entire length of the structure.

There is some machinery left at the top of the tower. Much of the machinery in the tower is rather precarious.

Right: Here is a model T owned by the owner of the grain silo.

Below: Another classic ford parked outside of the grain silo. This specific one is a model A.

6

FORGOTTEN VENTURES AND ROAD-SIDE ABANDONMENTS

Montana is covered in forgotten ventures and roadside abandonments. Deep in the mountains, there are a slew of mining camps, rotted and collapsed. In many cases, they lasted less than a decade. A mine was dug and a wooden headframe constructed, but operations just couldn't last. Whether it was a lack of profitability or longevity, no one knows. They never churned out the millions in ore that the more well-known ghost towns did. Maybe a couple of houses or cabins were built, but they were far from a "town." Now, all that is left is the off-kilter headframe and a selection of shacks, miner's quarters, and sheds. All one can do is walk around the remnants and conceive their own stories.

The abandoned stores, grain silos, and barns that are visible off of weather-beaten highways are equally as interesting. Some have stories, like a failed flour production venture or a forgotten radio station, but others leave it to the mind's creativity. Who knows why a large piece of construction equipment sits outside a small cabin in the woods or why there are piles and piles of bingo cards in a shed. One can't go to any town in Montana and not see these peculiar places, so why not pull over and take a couple of quick snapshots of these structures before they are truly forgotten and gone?

Right: Montana is covered in abandoned railroad tunnels. This tunnel is near Butte on a hiking trail.

Below: This grain silo is just off of the highway towards Lewistown. The surrounding fields are simply beautiful.

Left: Here is another view of the grain silo. It has a fitting name, "Montana Elevator Co."

Below: Near Elliston Montana, there is a myriad of abandoned cabins buried deep in the woods. This cabin still has clothes on the line and pots and pans in the kitchen.

This large piece of construction equipment is outside the cabin, a rather strange placement of such a machine.

About two miles up a forest service road, there is a beautiful valley with this mill. It is mostly collapsed, but it is very interesting, nonetheless.

Almost comically, there is a roof and windows, but very little in the realm of walls. It certainly lets in a lot of natural light.

This is the second floor of a miner's quarters, although most of the side has fallen away.

Right: This International Harvester dump truck is sitting in a field amongst rotting cabins. With an engine that rusted, it's certainly not going to run any time soon.

Below: A tree sits on top of this cabin. Luckily, it is still standing, although it seems to be sinking into the ground.

Above: This forest house has no roof, but it does have a beautiful view of a stream and an abandoned headframe and cabins.

Left: Nearby, there is an abandoned car. It is painted green and is full of bullet holes. It is hard to tell what type of car it is, due to the damage.

Right: A window of an abandoned cabin has a great view into the forest.

Below: This small cabin is one of the cabins in the view of the mountain house. Oddly enough, its fireplace is twenty feet away in a field.

Off the road, near Moccasin, sits an abandoned gas station. Its walls read "Rat Kid."

Off the side of a highway, in the Highline of Montana, sits this church with a sort of pueblo style. It has a very colorful graveyard to its side.

Above left: Near a very small lake, there are a couple of cabins. This particular white cabin has a very pretty covered porch.

Above right: Inside the house, there is a very dated IBM computer. The carpet seems to be made of a spattering of random carpet clippings sewn together.

Left: A quaint little barn with a half door has a great view of this pond. The front of this building is in relatively good shape, but the rear is almost completely collapsed.

Below: There is so much green in such a small space. Just out of view in the grass, there is a fridge tipped over that had been filled with random cans.

Right: Just off a highway, this grain elevator towered above the surrounding stores. It looks as if this "General Ranch Supplies" building had an extension that was demolished.

Below: The old KPRK radio station building is just down the road from the grain elevator. It has a very interesting space-age spire on its front door.

Left: Here is a better look at the beautiful retro styling.

Below: In a shed behind the radio station, there are piles and piles of bingo cards. These bingo cards lay in front of a pile of rubbish and other game pieces.

7

MONTANA STATE ORPHANAGE

Visible just off Highway 24, the former Montana State Orphanage looms over nearby Twin Bridges. In 1894, a large Victorian house known as the "Castle" was constructed to house a growing number of destitute children. Most that passed through the orphanage were not "true" orphans, rather their parents, often single or widowed mothers, had no means to support them. This trend was at its height during the Great Depression when the orphanage housed 282 children on average. For this very reason, it was a favorite local charity.

Common donations from the Copper Kings and other rich businessmen allowed for lavish expansions. The orphans had an indoor pool, a theater with a projector room, a large gymnasium, a shop for learning trades, etc. Through all these amenities, the Montana State Orphanage made big on its promise to provide each of its children with all the necessary tools to have productive adult lives.

It did so with very strict rules and guidelines, however. Criticism of orphanages stated that abuse was commonplace in many of the institutions. According to the recollection of its residents, the Montana State Orphanage was no different. If nothing else, it was at least quite harsh. Francis R. Murphy recalls "being forever afraid of the dark after being repeatedly locked in a dark cloakroom."[1] This is one of a multitude of jarring stories.

In 1959, the Montana State Orphanage rebranded itself as the Montana State Children's Home in an attempt to distance itself from traditional orphanages and rather a home for foster children. Following this decision, it adopted a "cottage" system to make the orphanage more like a home instead of an institution. At this time, fewer and fewer children were finding themselves in the Montana State Children's Home, and the average number of orphans had fallen to 156. Public support was still waning, however, even with the rebranding and restructuring of the home. In 1975, when only fifty children remained, the Montana State Children's Home closed its doors for good. Over the period of its eighty-one-year life, the Montana State Orphanage had been home to over 5000 children. Since then, it has switched hands many times. Occasional repairs have been made, but the complex is still far from its original glory. Creaky floors, covered in the rubble of what was once a roof, leave an eerie feeling. The orphanage has become orphaned; Mother Nature has become its foster parent.

Right: The "Castle" sits in the center of a swath of red buildings. It has a beautiful turret and porch, but it is leaning quite substantially.

Below: This is one of the many "cottages" dotted around the campus. Its lawn is overgrown and unkept.

Above left: A very prominent feature of the Twin Bridges Orphanage is its water tower. This particular door is the back door of the machine shop.

Above right: The machine shop connects up to the boiler building. The interior of the boiler building is still completely furnished with curtains on the windows.

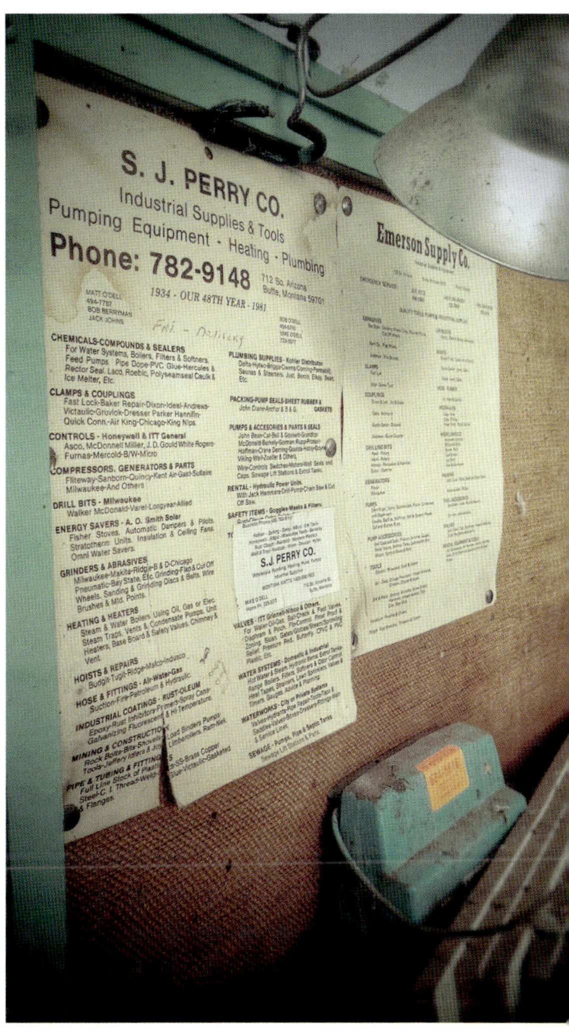

Above left: Two large boilers were used to heat the entirety of the Montana State Orphanage. The entire room is filled with pipes.

Above right: In a side room, it is evident that nothing has changed since the complex's original abandonment. These phone numbers for maintenance have been here for forty years.

Left: On the property, there is a '40s Mack flatbed truck. There are so many dials, buttons, and switches in the truck.

Below: All the cottages in the complex are almost identical. This is the rear of one of the cottages that border the Castle.

Above left: These uneven cracked sidewalks carve through the complex. The sidewalks have steam lines to heat buildings underneath them.

Above right: These fire alarm pull stations are placed on the outside of every building. They stand out with their bright yellow paint against red bricks.

Above: This extension on the rear of the main school building houses a large open theater area.

Left: This is one of the many window views out of the stage area.

Right: The bathroom inside of the school is still relatively intact. Only the paint is peeling and fading.

Below: One can see the age of this building by simply looking at the retro overhead lights in this classroom, not to mention the very bright yellow lead paint.

Above: This building sat in a small field. Inside, there is a water main, likely for the nearby recreational building that has a pool.

Left: Out of the buildings in the complex, the recreational building is the worst for wear. This hallway has exposed brick walls and a crumbling roof.

Right: At one point, it seems that this pool had a roof. Those days have passed and now weeds are sprouting at the bottom.

Below: For such a grand arch, the building is quite small. It appeared to have been used as a classroom at one point in its life.

8

THE MONTANA STATE DEAF AND DUMB ASYLUM

Scattered remnants of the old Montana Deaf and Dumb Asylum can be seen from Main St. in Boulder. Before Montana had even reached statehood, territorial governor Preston Leslie requested funds for the creation of a deaf and dumb asylum. In 1889, 50,000 acres were acquired to fundraise for the asylum's creation. However, proper funds would not be obtained till 1893 when the legislature provided additional monetary aid. Until the structure's completion in 1898, the asylum resided in a small frame house or the second story of a local store, both in Boulder. In 1902, an addition to the original Deaf and Dumb asylum was made to house the School for the Feeble-Minded. The so-called "feeble-minded children" were moved from the Montana State Insane Asylum to Boulder, following a decision by the legislature. It deemed that feeble-minded children had the susceptibility to become insane while enrolled in the Insane Asylum.

All of these names are very unfortunate by today's standards, but even then they were not well received. In a 1902 report, the superintendent of the Deaf and Dumb Asylum urged a name change, stating that the name "was not only a misnomer but also a source of injury to our work."[1] The following year, the name was amended to the "Montana School for the Deaf and Dumb," a much more fitting name for an educational institution. Over a short period of time, many new buildings were constructed, particularly the establishment of the Montana Training School for Feeble-Minded and Backward Children in 1905.

When the deaf and blind department moved to Great Falls Montana in 1937, the entire facility was transferred to the Montana Training School for Feeble-Minded and Backward Children and renamed simply as the Montana State Training School. As time wore on, the original Deaf and Dumb Asylum building became used as storage.

In 1976, the 1902 addition was demolished to accommodate new construction and return the building to its original design. Of the few remaining original buildings, none have been maintained. Plans have been made to restore the Deaf and Dumb Asylum, but the building is in a sorry state. The basement walls have buckled over time, and one can see through holes in the foundation. The Training School for Feeble-Minded and Backwards Children building has become a haven for pigeons and owls. Few windows have not been knocked out by thrill-seeking teenagers. The local granite from which they were built slowly sinks back into the earth.

Above: The old Deaf and Dumb Asylum building is emblazoned with a plaque reading, "The Montana State Training School," the last name that the building's complex had before the building stopped being used.

Left: Its Italianate architecture makes the building particularly beautiful and interesting.

Right: It towers over the nearby buildings in all of its nearly four stories.

Below: The school housed two small concrete boxes in the basement that could be deemed "fallout shelters."

Above left: The hallway double-door that leads to what was the front door, now a heavy wall of boards, is a bright blue.

Above right: The entire building had been stripped of anything that could be moved or removed easily, leaving so many empty rooms like this one.

Above left: This very interesting set of doors does not open at all and has a large bookshelf behind them.

Above right: The only things left in the old Deaf and Dumb Asylum are the mirrors, sinks, and other bathroom appliances. This sink and mirror are dirty but undamaged.

Many of the windows, including these, have a very odd discoloration. They are white and hazed over.

There are two stairwells on either side of the building. This particular section of the stairwell is one of the only ones without one of its windows boarded up.

Above left: The entire attic had either caved in or been removed due to water damage, leaving an eerie glow of the top window that bled through where a floor once was.

Above right: The top floor has few functioning windows and even fewer non-crumbling sections of the floor.

Left: For no apparent reason, this door led from one entrance of the school into a closet and then into an adjacent classroom.

Below: This building is across the river from the Deaf and Dumb Asylum and was the original Training School for Feeble-Minded and Backward Children.

9

ST. MARIE

Just off Highway 24, three water towers interrupt flat plains as far as the eye can see. A sign that reads "Welcome to St. Marie: Home of the Adventurous" creaks dryly in the wind. Just seventeen miles north from Glasgow, MT, lies what used to be the Glasgow Air Force Base, or AFB, and what is now a small town by the name of St. Marie. Construction began in 1955 and the Glasgow AFB was opened in 1957, under the Air Defense Command. In 1960, the base was turned over to the Strategic Air Command or the SAC and the base's runways were lengthened to accommodate much larger bombers and tankers. As the base expanded, its supporting town of St. Marie grew in population.

At its height, St. Marie was home to over 7,000 people. The housing itself was built to accommodate up to 10,000. For its residents, it had K-12 education across multiple schools, a movie theater, a bowling alley, a full-size hospital, etc. Sadly, the base's prospects would be short-lived, and the Glasgow AFB would be shut down in 1968, after only eleven years of operation.

Following the closure, 16,000 people would leave the area. Briefly, in 1971, the base would be opened again only to close five years later in 1976. After sitting dormant for many years, Boeing would acquire the base for use as a testing ground for aviation projects, testing that still goes on today. St. Marie itself, however, was left devastated after the Glasgow AFB's initial closure.

The actual name of "St. Marie" was coined by a retired Air Force officer, Patrick Kelly, in tribute to his daughter, when he attempted to create a veteran retirement community out of the desolate town in the 1980s. He purchased much of the properties by paying their overdue property taxes but eventually would fail to maintain tax payments himself. Later down the line in 2012, Terry Lee Brauner and Merrill

Leon Frantz attempted to create a "sovereign citizen" enclave by purchasing the vast majority of the abandoned property, again through paying back taxes, in St. Marie. Sovereign citizens, simply put, do not believe that the United States government has a legitimate rule and are flagged as domestic terrorists by the FBI. They were met with fierce resistance by the townspeople, as the sovereigns took a hostile approach to their integration into the town. They pursued eminent domain and various tries at homeowners' associations in an attempt to oust the St. Marie residents from their own homes, along with threats towards the aforementioned, Pat Kelly.

Today, despite the colorful history of property ownership in the town, little has been done to the properties themselves. They sit with open doors and broken windows, collapsed roofs, and crumbling foundations. Only 212 of the nearly 1,000 original houses are inhabited. Most of the duplexes are vacant. The fourplexes sit, almost comically, with one section missing paint, windows, or any semblance of upkeep, and on the other side of the wall lies a house with freshly painted walls, a mowed lawn, and a bustling family. For urban explorers, abandoned buildings are a hobby or a passion; for those who inhabit St. Marie, they are simply a part of life. The tarnished houses, schools, and shops are pictures framed neatly in windows, a room acting as a scrapbook of days gone by.

In St. Marie, a street with houses like this, with doors ajar, broken windows, and peeling paint, is very common.

This garage is propped open, displaying an overgrown driveway and similarly ransacked houses.

Above left: If it is not glaringly apparent, these very abandoned neighborhoods are labeled with "out of service" labels on their fire hydrants with peeling paint. All fire alarms in the area have similar warnings.

Above right: This fridge full of food has been left for who knows how long. There is a bowl of black and a plate of mush brown.

Right: Each house seemed to have a similar supply of these flower print chairs in their garages—strange.

Below: At least there is a playground among all this doom and gloom.

Left: It is unknown what is in this bottle, how long it has been there, and why it was put on a roundabout.

Below: This unknown trailer is oddly ornate for its purpose. The trailer jack in front of it points to recent repairs, however.

A scene of such abandonment is surreal in the real world. It would be more fitting in a zombie movie or a post-apocalyptic video game.

It is unknown what is Montana's obsession with shooting junk cars in fields. This yellow truck is no different.

These fourplexes sit much like the other scenes, a water tower in the distance and driveways overgrown.

It is simply bizarre to be inside a completely empty movie theater. This single theater had light filtering into the projection area, creating an odd sort of movie.

Right: This mop and bucket were likely left when the theater closed and have not moved since.

Below: One would have to squint to even see a semblance of a parking lot in front of this hospital.

Left: These vaguely threatening "no trespassing" signs are plastered all over any of the properties owned by sovereign citizens.

Below: Every bed is crammed haphazardly into rooms; some are even left in the hallways.

Above left: Another bed, this time from a different era, is parked in yet another dilapidated room. This room has tattered drapes and a collapsing ceiling.

Above right: There are multiple operating rooms with gigantic lights in the hospital. Other than the light, this room is completely bare.

There are very few large windows that are not smashed like this one in the hospital.

Just across the street from the hospital is a ramshackle school. Certainly, no buses are stopping near here anymore.

The gymnasium is the only structurally stable part of the school. Due to its durable construction, however, it is home to a lot of pigeons.

No hallway is safe from roof damage or outright collapse. This hallway is in fairly sturdy shape in comparison to the others.

If this school could be described in one word, that word would be tetanus. However much one would like to watch out of the bay windows, one must look at their feet in caution.

This front entrance of the school could hardly even be deemed indoors as the sky is visible in every direction.

ENDNOTES

CHAPTER 1

1. Lincoln, M., "Comet Ghost Town: Silent Witness to a Thunderous Past," *Helena Independent Record* (September 9, 2007)

CHAPTER 5

1. "Flour Mills Completed: The Montana Flour Mills Co. Finishes Best Plant in State At Harlowton," *The Harlowton News* (A. H. Eislein: Harlowton, 1912)

CHAPTER 7

1. Stripling, S., "Memories of the Orphanage—Two Men Relive Their Days at a Montana Home and Give New Insight Into a National Debate," *The Seattle Times*, (July 21, 1995)

CHAPTER 8

1. McAloney, T., "Deaf and Dumb Asylum," *Annual Report of the State Board of Education of the State of Montana*, pp. 130-138 (Helena, Montana: State Pub. Co. 1902)

BIBLIOGRAPHY

Contract Let: Van Busrick & Dunnigan Awarded Contract to Construct Big Flour Mill," *The Harlowton News*, (A. H. Eislein: Harlowton, 1909)

"Elkhorn Montana," *Western Mining History*

FBI Counterterrorism Analysis Section, "Sovereign Citizens A Growing Domestic Threat to Law Enforcement," Federal Bureau of Investigation (2011)

"Flour Mills Completed: The Montana Flour Mills Co. Finishes Best Plant in State At Harlowton," *The Harlowton News*, (A. H. Eislein: Harlowton, 1912)

Lenz, R., "Fear and Loathing in Montana," *Southern Poverty Law Center* (2016)

Lincoln, M., "Comet Ghost Town: Silent Witness to a Thunderous Past," *Helena Independent Record* (2007)

McAloney, T., "Deaf and Dumb Asylum," *Annual Report of the State Board of Education of the State of Montana*, pp. 130-138 (Helena, Montana: State Pub. Co. 1902)

"Milwaukee Railroads," *Upper Musselshell Museum*

National Park Service, "National Register of Historic Places Inventory–Nomination Form," (1980)

Nicholes, E., "Castle Town epitomizes Montana's vanishing ghost towns," *Bozeman Daily Chronicle* (2004)

Person, D., "A Place Where History Stands Still," *Bozeman Daily Chronicle* (2010)

Strategic Air Command, "SAC Bases: Glasgow Air Force Base"

Stripling, S., "Memories of the Orphanage– Two Men Relive Their Days at a Montana Home and Give New Insight Into a National Debate," *The Seattle Times* (1995)

"The Milwaukee Road, "Route of the Hiawatha's"," *American Rails* (2021)

The Montana National Register Sign Program, "Milwaukee Road Substation #10 (Primrose Station)," *Historic Montana*

"There's No Place Like Home: The Role of the Montana State Orphanage," *Montana Women's History* (2014)

Therriault, E., "St. Marie: Montana's Newest Ghost Town," *Distinctly Montana* (2020)

Weiser-Alexander, K., "Castle Town, Montana," *Legends of America* (2020)

Weiser-Alexander, K., "Comet – Silent on the Eastern Slope," *Legends of America* (2021)

Weiser-Alexander, K., "Elkhorn, Montana Survives Today," *Legends of America* (2019)

[*Photo by Colten Grandy*]